NINJA KID 6

NINJA GIANTS!

Scholastic Press
An imprint of Scholastic Australia Pty Limited (ABN 11 000 614 577)
PO Box 579 Gosford NSW 2250
www.scholastic.com.au

Part of the Scholastic Group
Sydney • Auckland • New York • Toronto • London • Mexico City
• New Delhi • Hong Kong • Buenos Aires • Puerto Rico

First published by Scholastic Australia in 2020.

A catalogue record for this book is available from the National Library of Australia

Typeset in Bizzle-Chizzle, featuring Hola Bisou and Handblock.

ISBN 978-93-5471-900-4

This reprint edition: November 2025

Printed in India at MicroPrints India, New Delhi

ANH DO

illustrated by Anton Emdin

NINJA KID 6

NINJA GIANTS!

A Scholastic Press book
from Scholastic Australia

ONE

My name is **Nelson Kane**. For the first nine years of my life, I was just an average, everyday NERD.

I used to read the dictionary **for fun!**

Then when I turned ten, I developed **ninja powers!** Now, whenever I need to use those powers, I become . . .

NiNJA KiD!

My ninja abilities came from my **dad**, who went missing when I was just a baby.

I'm only now starting to work out what **happened** to him.

I live in a **junkyard** with my **mum**, my **grandma** and my **cousin Kenny**. Kenny's secret identity is **H-DUDE** - my funny, always hungry **sidekick.**

Grandma is a world-famous `inventor`. Well, maybe not **'world famous'** but she's definitely my **favourite** inventor!

We live in **Duck Creek**, which used to be the most **peaceful** town around.

But lately, Duck Creek has been the total **opposite** of peaceful!

And it's all because of one man - my dad's **twin** brother,

ANDREW KANE.

Just like me, my dad got his **ninja powers** when he turned ten. But Andrew didn't get any powers at all! And that made him **burn** with anger.

Grandma taught Andrew everything she knew about inventing. When Andrew grew up, he stole Grandma's inventions and **left** Duck Creek.

Now he's back as **DOCTOR KANE** and he wants everyone to leave Duck Creek so he can mine it for rare **hypno diamonds**.

H-Dude and Ninja Kid have managed to **Stop** all of Dr Kane's attempts to take over Duck Creek, so we're right at the top of his list of **'MOST HATED THINGS'**.

Dr Kane has become **obsessed** with finding out Ninja Kid's true **identity**. Despite all his attempts to unmask us, Kenny and I have managed to keep our **identities** a secret.

Now, Kenny and I are taking on **new identities** . . .

. . . for HALLOWEEN!

The scariest and most fun time of the year!

TWO

In most places, Halloween is about **trick or treating**. But in Duck Creek, it's all about the **Halloween Fair!**

The Halloween Fair is the **BIGGEST** event on the Duck Creek calendar. We look forward to it every year!

The fair always has **heaps** of fun carnival games, food stalls and cool rides!

Last year, Kenny and I still weren't tall enough to go on the scariest (and best) rides like

The NanaConda...

Or THE SPOOKY SPEW-MAKER...

Or THE HOWLING WEREWOLF!

Since last **Halloween Fair**, Kenny and I have slept well and eaten all our veggies (most of the time), hoping that by the time the fair returned, we'd be **TALL** enough for ALL the scariest rides.

We even took on a **TOUGH** exercising program!

Kenny was a **hard** fitness trainer. When I was so **exhausted** I could hardly move, he'd make me do ten extra **push-ups!**

We even spent ten minutes every day hanging off the monkey bars, hoping that it would **streeeeeeeeeetch** us!

We waited until the day before the Halloween Fair to **measure** ourselves. But the ruler brought **terrible** news!

Luckily, we had a back-up plan . . .

hair gel!

Now that we were **juuuuust** tall enough, we were **super excited** to get to the fair. Kenny gets even hungrier when he's excited.

'Can I have that **Spare** bowl of porridge, too?' Kenny asked.

'It's not a spare,' Mum said. 'It's Grandma's breakfast!'

'Where is Grandma?' I asked.

'She's having storage issues in her workshop so she's doing a tidy up,' Mum said. 'I'm sure she'd love some help.'

'And we'd love to give her a helping hand or four,' Kenny said, 'but we can't be late for the bus to the **Halloween Fair!** Byeeeee!'

'Wait, Kenny! We need to say goodbye to Grandma!' I reminded him.

'But she'll make us help clean the workshop!' Kenny said.

'It's the least we can do after all the great things she's done for us! C'mon, it'll be fun.'

'You're right,' Kenny replied. 'And the last time I saw Grandma's workshop it was in pretty good shape. Won't take us long.'

Kenny spoke **WAAAAAY** too soon!

There were boxes scattered all over the floor. There were bits of metal and

timber everywhere. There were hundreds of **half-finished inventions** piled on top of each other!

Like the family **haircutting machine . . .**

And the glow-in-the-dark toilet!

'Hi, Grandma, we're here to help you clean up the workshop!' I said.

'Thanks for the offer,' Grandma said. 'But it's all sorted. Check this out.'

'Whoa! What's that?' I asked.

'You'll see!' Grandma replied. She **aimed** the device at the glow-in-the-dark toilet and **fired!**

The toilet **shrank** to **HALF** its size!

Next, Grandma aimed the device at the boxes on the floor.

The boxes shrunk down to **miniature** versions of themselves, allowing Grandma to easily stack them on the shelves.

Grandma kept **firing** until there was nothing left on the floor.

'That is seriously impressive!' I said.

'So it's a shrink gun?' Kenny asked.

'No,' Grandma replied. 'It's a `size converter`. It can make things **bigger,** too.'

'Can you please make my brain bigger?' Kenny asked. 'I'd love to be SMART enough to win a quiz show!'

'There's no shortcut to intelligence,' Grandma replied. 'And your brain is the **perfect size** for your head!'

'Speaking of heads, I'm **heading** inside to eat my porridge. Have a brilliant day at the Halloween Fair, boys,' Grandma said.

'Will do!' Kenny and I replied together.

'Oh, and one more thing,' Grandma said. '**Don't touch** the `size converter`. It's still got some **kinks** that need to be ironed out.'

'We won't go anywhere near it,' I said.

'Have a great day, Grandma!' Kenny added.

'Are you thinking what I'm thinking?' Kenny asked me.

'Let's get going so we can get the best seats on the Halloween Fair bus?'

'Who cares about good seats when we won't be able to go on any of the good rides?'

'What are you talking about? Our hair-gel plan is foolproof!'

'Foolproof?! Your hair's already **sagging**, Nelson! You look like an alpaca after a bad day at the hairdresser!'

'I have a better plan,' Kenny said. 'If we **ZAP** each other with the `size converter` on the **"SMiDGE BiGGeR"** setting, we'll be tall enough for ALL the rides!'

'Grandma told us not to touch it,' I said. 'And we agreed.'

'**You** agreed,' Kenny said. 'I didn't say a word.'

'Hmmm . . . still, it doesn't feel right.'

'Do you know what doesn't feel right? Missing out at the Halloween Fair AGAIN!'

I'm not sure if it was the excitement about the fair, but Kenny was extra **convincing** today!

'Alright,' I said, 'but we're zapping ourselves straight back after the fair.'

'Of course we are!' Kenny said. 'Now stand still.'

'Hang on! Why do I get **zapped** first?'

'Because you promised Grandma you wouldn't touch the size converter!' Kenny replied.

'No, no, no,' I said. 'The only fair way to do this is for **both of us** to get **zapped** at the same time.'

'Fine!' Kenny said. He turned the dial to the **'SMIDGE BIGGER'** setting and bunched up next to me.

NOOOOO!

THREE

'Kenny, what have you done?!' I squeaked.

'I must have bumped the dial when I turned the size converter around!' Kenny replied in a tiny voice.

'You need to **ZAP** us back to normal size,' I said. '**Now!**'

'I can't!' Kenny squeaked. 'My **tiny** hands aren't strong enough to move the dial!'

'We need to go and get Grandma,' I said. 'She'll be able to **ZAP** us back!'

We hurried out of the workshop as fast as our tiny feet would take us.

Which was **NOT very fast!**

We'd only just stepped outside when suddenly an enormous **shadow** loomed over us . . .

WHOOOOSH!

It was a **crow!** A SWOOPING crow!

Kenny and I **Sprinted** as fast as we could, but we weren't quick enough to **escape** the crow. It was about to **scoop** me up in its beak . . .

. . . when mini-Kenny shouted, **'Jump in here!'**

It was **dark** and **dirty** inside the old toaster. Kenny and I were **sweating** like crazy as the crow stuck its beak into the bread slots, trying to **peck** us.

It must have thought we were massive **worms!**

Luckily, the crow's beak wasn't long enough to reach us. After what seemed like an eternity, it finally gave up and **flew away.**

Kenny and I climbed out of the toaster.

'I like being scared on **Halloween**, but that was ridiculous!' I said.

'Right now, everything is **scary!**' said Kenny. 'Even a giant donut wouldn't make me feel any better!'

We had to make it back to the house before another terrifying creature struck.

'A praying mantis!' Kenny squealed. 'And it looks in a **bad mood!**'

Even though praying mantises aren't super quick, we knew its long legs would make it much quicker than us. Luckily, we found a remote-control car nearby and jumped in!

'Accelerate!' Kenny yelled.

It took all my strength to push the toggle forward. It worked!

We drove around the praying mantis - it couldn't believe its **beady** eyes!

We'd only just escaped the praying mantis when we ran smack into a new **threat!**

'Go left!' I yelled to Kenny.

'Alright!' Kenny said.

'No left!' I said.

Kenny pushed the button left and we hurtled up an old piece of wood. We used the wood as a ramp, **jumping high** over the lawnmower and landing on a soft patch of grass.

The longer we were in the tiny car, the better we got at controlling it.

We **dodged**, **weaved** and ***darted*** our way through the junkyard until finally we arrived at our front door. It looked

ENORMOUS!

We were so small we could fit **underneath** the door!

We jumped out of the car and ran inside.

As we raced towards the kitchen, we were almost stomped on by a **GIANT!**

Grandma's foot stopped only millimetres from our heads. She didn't look very happy to see us.

'I told you not to touch the size converter!' Grandma said. 'You boys really need to start listening to me.'

'It was all my fault,' Kenny squeaked.

'Mine too,' I added.

'It's very disappointing you didn't listen to Grandma. Again!' said Mum.

Mum hardly ever got angry with us. We felt **terrible.**

'Let's get you back to the workshop and back to normal size,' Grandma sighed. 'Jump on.'

When we got back to the workshop, Grandma grabbed the size converter and twisted the dial to **'GINORMOUS'**.

Kenny and I were **trembling** in our tiny goblin boots as she **fired** at us.

ZAP!

It **half** worked! We were bigger again ... but we were only **half** our normal size!

'Grandma, we're only **half** the goblins we used to be!' I said.

'We won't even be allowed on the **merry-go-round** like this!' Kenny wailed.

'I did tell you the size converter had **kinks** that needed ironing out,' Grandma said. 'Give me a second.' Grandma picked up the size converter and **banged** it hard on her desk. 'Let's try it again,' she said with confidence. 'Stand still!'

PPPPP!

This time, **nothing** happened! We were still half our size!

'I can't believe banging it on the desk didn't fix it, Grandma!' Kenny said.

Grandma was studying the `size converter`. 'Here's our problem,' she said. 'The battery has run out!'

'How long does it take to **recharge**?' I asked.

'Should be back to full power by this afternoon,' Grandma replied.

This AFTERNOON???!!!

'We can't go to the Halloween Fair like this!' I said.

'Sure you can! It just looks like you're **crouching** down!'

'What about our tiny **heads?!'** Kenny asked.

'I have a solution for that,' Grandma said. 'Where did I put them . . . ?'

Kenny and I fidgeted as Grandma searched her now very tidy workshop.

'Here they are!' Grandma announced. 'These will make your heads look bigger.'

FOUR

We were running **late** so there was no time to argue with Grandma. Mum dropped us off at school, half our normal size, with fishbowls on our heads!

Everyone had put a ton of effort into their Halloween costumes.

Sarah looked super cool as a **vampire bat.**

Tiffany looked awesome as a **scary pirate.**

Billy Bob made a great **SCARECROW.**

Charles Brock dressed up as our teacher, Mr Fletcher. And he looked just like him!

And **Mr Fletcher** was dressed as the least scary **clown** ever!

But, as amazing as everyone's costumes were, Kenny and I still stood out like **sore thumbs!** Very small sore thumbs!

'How did you guys make yourselves so small?' Sarah asked.

'It's just an **illusion!**' I said.

'All smoke and mirrors!' Kenny added. 'It's not like we were zapped with a `size converter` or anything!'

'Well . . .' Sarah said, sizing us up. 'I think you both look utterly **brilliant!**'

'Best dressed for sure,' Tiffany agreed.

As we **piled** onto the bus, Sarah tapped me on the shoulder. 'Can I sit next to you, space goblin Nelson?'

My tiny goblin legs turned to jelly!

'Of course!' I replied in a voice that was much higher than I'd hoped.

'Can I sit next to you, space goblin Kenny?' Tiffany asked.

'Absolutely!' Kenny replied.

Maybe being **bite-sized** wasn't so bad after all!

'Halloween's my **favourite** time of the year,' I said to Sarah.

'Mine too,' Sarah said. 'It reminds me of my **dad**. He took me to the Halloween Fair every year. He was so good at carnival games. I'd always go home with my arms full of **prizes** he'd won for me.'

Sarah's voice sounded sad.

'Doesn't your dad take you to the **Halloween Fair** anymore?' I asked.

Sarah shook her head. 'He works overseas now. I only get to see him a few times a year.'

'I miss my dad, too,' I said. 'I don't remember ever going to the fair with him. He **disappeared** when I was a **baby.**'

'That's terrible,' Sarah said. 'I'm so sorry.'

'Don't be sorry. I think I've found out what's happened to him,' I told her. 'And I'm going to bring him home.'

'I really hope you do,' Sarah said.

She was really nice. I really liked Sarah a lot.

FiVE

When we arrived at the Halloween Fair, there was a huge sign at the front gates that made everyone even more **excited** than they already were!

The two new rides looked **out of this world!**

There was a mega-coaster called the **T-Rex Tail of Terror** . . .

And the **Ghastly Ghost Train!**

Wow, those rides were awesome! But Kenny and I were going to be too small to go on them . . . **again!**

Before we got to the rides, we had a go at the carnival games. I really wanted to win a prize for Sarah, like her dad used to do when they came to the fair.

But it turns out I was **really bad** at all the games! I used to be a master of the **dart and balloon** game, but now I was half my size and strength, my dart didn't even reach the wall!

Kenny had similar problems.

We couldn't even go mini-pumpkin bobbing! If we took the fishbowls off, everyone would see our tiny heads! So we just had to watch as everyone else had all the **fun**.

Of course, Charles Brock was winning everything!

He was so desperate to win the **WHACK-A-MOLE** game that he almost whacked me and Kenny!

'Let's go on the new **T-Rex** mega-coaster!' Tiffany said.

'Great idea!' Sarah replied.

Tiffany and Sarah led Kenny and I to the new ride before we had a chance to explain there was **no way** we'd be allowed on it!

The **T-Rex Tail of Terror** was **JAW DROPPING!** It was as huge as a real T-Rex! The twisty ride went up and down the T-Rex's back and tail, with an **'in the dark'** section in the T-Rex's mouth!

During the ride, the T-Rex **roared** and **stomped** its legs up and down, creating even more **scares**!

The roaring and stomping was activated by a guy in a **control booth** inside the T-Rex's right eye.

'I can't believe we're missing out on this,' I whispered to Kenny.

'We need to talk the ride attendant into letting us on,' Kenny said.

Sarah and Tiffany were already seated on the ride when Kenny and I reached the front of the queue.

'We've saved you seats, guys!' Sarah called out.

But the ride attendant had other ideas. 'You're **nowhere near tall enough,'** he said. 'Stop wasting my time.'

'Hey, goblin dweebs,' Charles hollered from behind us, 'if you're not going on the ride, step out of the line!'

'C'mon, Nelson and Kenny, quit messing around!' Sarah called out.

'Just **stand up properly** and get on!' Tiffany added.

Kenny and I couldn't think of anything more fun than going on a **CRAZY** new Halloween ride with Sarah and Tiffany.

Kenny tried his best. 'Hey, Caveman, that's a great outfit,' he said smoothly, 'you should do some prehistoric modelling.'

'It's not going to work, tiny space goblin,' the attendant replied. 'You're just too small.'

Kenny and I looked at each other and realised we had no chance.

We stepped out of the line and tried to walk as **tall** as we could.

'Have fun, everyone. We're going to get some goblicious popcorn!' Kenny called.

But the truth was we were **really disappointed** to be missing out.

Afterwards, everyone was talking about the T-Rex ride like it was the best thing they'd experienced in their lives!

And the **bad times** kept rolling.

Next, everyone headed to the other new ride, the **Ghastly Ghost Train.**

Above the entrance to the ride was a giant **robotic ghost**, which could actually **float** in the air! It was also controlled by a worker in a control booth, this time in the ghost's mouth.

The ghost had a basket full of **giant pumpkins** in its hand.

We didn't even bother lining up for the Ghastly Ghost Train. And Sarah and Tiffany didn't bother asking us to try.

The **Ghastly Ghost Train** started its journey outside, but then zoomed inside a tunnel, so Kenny and I couldn't see what was happening.

But we could hear everyone **screaming** and **squealing**, and then we saw their **excited** faces when they got off the ride.

Kenny and I were sick of watching everyone else have fun, so we convinced Sarah and Tiffany to go to the **HALL OF MIRRORS** next. There were no height restrictions there!

Walking around the Hall of Mirrors was the best Kenny and I had felt all day, because everyone looked **short** in the squish mirrors!

And Kenny and I looked **tall** in the stretch mirrors!

We finally felt like our old selves!

Kenny was feeling so happy he started **dancing** to the music playing in the hall. With his goblin costume and fishbowl on his head, Kenny's already strange dance moves looked even more **BIZARRE.**

Tiffany thought he was so **funny!**

Tiffany's laughter made Kenny dance even more **excitedly**. He was jumping around so much, the fishbowl **flew off** his head!

Kenny quickly grabbed the fishbowl and shoved it back on his head, but it was too late.

'**Kenny, your head's totally shrunk!** What happened?!' Tiffany asked, horrified.

'My head hasn't shrunk!' Kenny said. 'These mirrors just make everything look weird!'

'Yeah, I guess,' Tiffany said, not entirely convinced.

Kenny hurried over to me. 'Ah, I may have just blown our cover!' he said.

'You did a great job of thinking on your feet,' I replied. 'But let's get out of here before anything else goes wrong.'

Just as we were about to sneak out of the Hall of Mirrors, a **NINJA JUMPED IN FRONT OF US!**

The Hall of Mirrors was a **strange** place, but I didn't expect to see a **ninja!**

But it turned out the ninja was just a toy!

'I won this in the clown game,' Sarah said. 'I thought you might want it!'

I couldn't believe it. I wanted to win Sarah a prize, but she won **me** one instead! And why did she think I'd like a ninja toy? Did she know I was **Ninja Kid?**

'I thought it was cute and I wanted you to have it,' Sarah said, sounding a little **hurt**. 'Why does it always have to be the boy winning stuff for the girl?'

'It doesn't,' I said. 'I just wanted to win something for you like your dad used to.'

'It wasn't getting prizes that I loved,' Sarah explained. 'It was hanging out with Dad. Just like I love hanging out with you.'

'All these games and rides have made me **hungry,'** Sarah said. 'Want to get a snack?'

'Finally, someone's speaking my language!' Kenny interrupted. 'Come on, everyone, I could really go a **Halloween hotdog!'**

'Sure thing,' I agreed. 'And, ah, Sarah, just out of interest, how did you know I liked ninjas?'

'Everyone likes ninjas!' Sarah exclaimed.

SiX

Sarah and I were just about to exit the Hall of Mirrors when we heard a familiar sound coming from outside.

WUP! WUP! WUP!

We rushed out to see Dr Kane's **helicopter** hovering above the fair!

His sidekick, an evil **chipmunk** called **EINSTEIN**, was in the passenger seat and the **ULTIMATE NINJA** was hanging from underneath.

'I hope you're all enjoying the fair!' Dr Kane shouted down through his **megaphone**.

'Yes, we are, thanks!' Billy Bob replied.

'I was being **sarcastic!**' Dr Kane shouted back.

'If you thought those rides were scary,' Dr Kane boomed, 'wait until you see **this!**'

The **ULTIMATE NINJA** *leapt off* the helicopter, effortlessly executing a perfect **somersault** before **jumping** onto the head of the T-Rex ride. He climbed inside the control booth as the attendant ran off.

Now the Ultimate Ninja was in control of the T-Rex!

He made it **ROAR** loudly then **STOMP** several times. Then something truly bizarre happened.

The enormous dinosaur started

STOMPING TOWARDS US!

The ground **crumbled** underneath the T-Rex as it **crushed** everything in its path.

The Ultimate Ninja made the T-Rex take a giant bite out of the kiosk roof, destroying the hotdog maker AND the candy floss machine. It was Kenny's worst nightmare!

Meanwhile, Einstein the **chipmunk** had jumped inside the **giant ghost** and managed to steer it away from the **Ghastly Ghost Train . . .**

. . . to fly above our heads!

As the ghost **hovered** high above us, it reached into its basket and started throwing **giant pumpkins!**

Kenny and I managed to **dodge** the first few pumpkins, but the third pumpkin landed right in front of us, **splattering** everyone with pumpkin juice!

The two out-of-control giant robots were **scaring** all of the fairgoers away.

'That's it! **Run!**' Dr Kane shouted into his megaphone. 'Duck Creek is **no place** for any of you!'

It was **bizarre** watching all those people dressed in **creepy** Halloween costumes running for their lives.

'Where are Ninja Kid and H-Dude?' Sarah asked. 'They should be here by now!'

'Ah, maybe they've got other problems to deal with,' I said **awkwardly**.

'No, they'll be here,' Tiffany said. 'They never let us down.'

Kenny and I felt **terrible.** This would be the perfect time for us to transform into Ninja Kid and H-Dude, but we were **half** our normal size! How could we possibly defeat a **T-Rex** and a **Mega-Ghost?!**

Dr Kane was getting exactly what he wanted. The fair was almost empty. It looked like this time he was going to win.

Then a **van** screeched through the fairground . . .

It was Grandma's workshop on wheels!

Kenny and **I RAN** towards the van.

'Where are you going?' Sarah called.

'The candy floss machine got smashed by the T-Rex. Which means there's free candy floss!' Kenny said. 'We'll bring you back some!'

We **sprinted** our tired little legs towards Grandma.

Grandma was waiting for us outside her mobile workshop. 'Why are my two grandsons just standing there while these **ridiculous creatures** ruin the fair for everyone?'

'Because we're tiny!' I said.

'What can we do?' Kenny asked.

'Save the day!' Grandma said. 'Get into your Ninja Kid and H-Dude disguises!'

'But they'll be way **too BIG!'** I said.

'Not once I've zapped you with this!' Grandma said.

Kenny and I weren't exactly **excited** to see the size converter again. But we didn't have much choice.

The **ULTIMATE NINJA** and **EINSTEIN** were wreaking **havoc!**

When we got changed into our **NINJA KID** and **H-DUDE** outfits we looked ridiculous! We looked more like kids **dressing up** in their parents' clothes than heroes!

Grandma didn't give us a second to complain. She aimed the size converter at us.

But the converter **misfired** again . . .

BIG time!

We were now **TEN**

METRES TALL!!!

'**Whoa!**' I said. I didn't recognise my own voice; it was so loud and deep!

'**Double whoa!**' Kenny boomed. His voice was even deeper than mine was!

'Stop **whoa-ing** and stand still, you two,' Grandma shouted up to us. 'I'll shrink you back to normal size.'

'**No!**' I said. 'Leave us like this. If we want to have any chance of bringing that giant ghost and T-Rex under control, we need to be **GIANTS**, too!'

'You're probably right,' Grandma said. 'Just watch your step!'

'Will do!' I said. 'Let's go, **Humongous Dude**.'

'Right back at ya, **Ninja Giant!**'

SEVEN

As Kenny and I **stomped** our giant bodies towards the T-Rex and Mega-Ghost, the ground shook beneath our tree-trunk legs. The other kids looked up at us in **awe** and **disbelief**.

'Look! It's Ninja Kid and H-Dude!' said Sarah.

'You guys are **HUGE!'** Tiffany said.

'Yep!' Kenny replied. 'Let this be a lesson to **keep eating your veggies,** kids!'

It felt **incredible** being so **enormous.** It made Kenny even **hungrier** than normal.

He reached into the half-destroyed kiosk, grabbed the popcorn machine and emptied the entire contents into his mouth.

When Dr Kane saw us, his eyes almost **popped** out of his head. But he was quick to hide his concern and return to his wisecracking self. 'Ninja Kid and H-Dude, have you two been working out?'

'Nice of you to notice!' Kenny said.

'Well, you know what they say,' Dr Kane shouted. 'The **bigger** they are, the harder they **FALL!** Take them down, Ultimate Ninja and Einstein!'

Together, the T-Rex and Mega-Ghost ripped up a large chunk of the rollercoaster track and **swung** it in front of my ankles.

'Ninja Kid!' Kenny shouted. 'Watch your feet!'

But it was too late. I tripped over the track.

Being so enormous suddenly felt **awkward** and **clumsy.**

I was about to do the biggest **face plant** of my life, when Kenny shouted, 'Drop and give me ten, Nelson!'

Kenny had said this to me so many times during our exercise training that my arms moved into the **push-up** position without me even thinking about it!

The push-up broke my fall! But there was no time to celebrate. Just as H-Dude was helping me back to my feet, the Mega-Ghost threw a massive pumpkin at me!

I **headed** it away like it was a giant, juicy soccer ball.

The ghost **hurled** another giant pumpkin at Kenny's head, but Kenny caught it.

'You want to play catch?' he called out. **'Cool, let's play catch!'**

He **pelted** the pumpkin at the Mega-Ghost!

As H-Dude continued his **pumpkin fight** with Einstein the chipmunk, I had my hands full, too!

The Ultimate Ninja made the T-Rex execute a powerful **roundhouse kick.** As its giant leg **speared** towards me, I managed to jump over it and do a **sweep kick,** bringing the T-Rex's hulking mechanical frame to the ground.

While the Ultimate Ninja struggled to get the T-Rex back on its feet, Kenny was teasing the Mega-Ghost. 'You're running out of pumpkins!' he shouted.

'But I've saved the **best till last,'** Einstein replied, hurling one more pumpkin at H-Dude.

Kenny ducked just in time - when the pumpkin hit the ground, it **exploded!**

It was a **PUMPKIN BOMB!**

Kenny and I stared in disbelief at the huge hole in the ground.

'Ninja Giant, remind me never to go trick or treating at that angry chipmunk's house!' Kenny said.

Kenny was so busy cracking jokes, he didn't see the second pumpkin attack hurtling towards him.

The pumpkin was about to strike H-Dude in the back! I quickly put each of my feet into dodgem cars, like they were giant metal shoes, then I **kicked** the pumpkin bomb back at the ghost's head.

Just seconds before the pumpkin was about to blow the control booth apart, Einstein shot into the sky on an **ejector seat!**

'So long, suckers!' he screeched at us.

Dr Kane caught Einstein in a **net** and lifted him into the safety of the helicopter.

'That was pathetic,' Dr Kane shouted at him. 'You're the worst sidekick ever! You're **all side** and **no kick!** You're a **SIDELOSER!**'

'Easy for you to criticise,' Einstein responded. 'All you've done is sit in a helicopter!'

'We'll talk about this later!' Dr Kane yelled. 'Get in!'

The chipmunk clambered into the passenger seat.

'Nice work, Ninja Giant!' Kenny was holding up his hand to high five me.

'H-Dude! Jump!' I yelled out.

But it was too late. The T-Rex swung its giant tail at Kenny's legs, causing him to fall **hard** onto the concrete ground.

Before I could go and check H-Dude was OK, the T-Rex whipped its tail at me, and I **crashed** to the ground.

'Cop that, **Injure Kid** and **H-Dud!'** Dr Kane yelled through his megaphone. 'Finish them, Ultimate Ninja!'

The Ultimate Ninja nodded, and the T-Rex **stomped** towards Kenny and me. Its giant feet were just about to squash us when suddenly . . . there were **hundreds** of us!

Tiffany, Sarah and the other kids from our class, had made it impossible for the **Ultimate Ninja** to work out who was the real **Ninja Giant** and **H-Dude**!

The clever mirror trick gave me enough time to get to my feet.

I jumped up and **punched** the control booth. The Ultimate Ninja came **flying out,** his arms and legs flailing as he tumbled towards the ground at great speed.

Even though the **ULTIMATE NINJA** had been trying to defeat us, I knew he had been **microchipped** by Dr Kane and he wasn't thinking for himself.

I also had a very strong feeling he was **my dad.**

I dived and **threw** out my hand to catch him. I managed to break the Ultimate Ninja's fall, but he **bounced off** my giant palm and landed hard on the ground.

As the Ultimate Ninja got to his feet, his hand went to his shoulder and he **grimaced.**

‘Is your shoulder OK?’ I asked.

The Ultimate Ninja didn’t reply, he just stared into my eyes. And in that moment, I was sure he was my **father.**

‘Dad . . . ?’ I said.

The Ultimate Ninja was about to respond when Dr Kane **swooped** down and pulled him into the helicopter.

'This isn't the end, Ninja Kid!' Dr Kane shouted down through his megaphone. 'I'll be back, **bigger** and **stronger!** And Duck Creek will be **all mine!**'

I knelt down to check on Kenny.

'H-Dude, are you alright?'

Kenny's eyes remained closed as he lay motionless on the ground. I began to panic.

Then he slowly opened his eyes. 'Don't suppose you have any giant headache tablets?' Kenny asked.

I helped Kenny back to his feet.

Even though Dr Kane had lost again, this time I felt like I had **lost** something, too.

Sarah and Tiffany rushed over to us.

'That was an **ENORMOUS** effort!' Sarah said.

'HUMONGOUS!' Tiffany said.

'We definitely couldn't have done it without you guys,' Kenny said.

'Yeah,' I said. 'That mirror trick was **genius!'**

We were interrupted by a horn **BEEPING**. It was the school bus!

'We have to go,' Tiffany said, running off. 'If you see Nelson and Kenny, tell them the bus is about to leave without them.'

'And that they've missed all the action,' Sarah said. 'Again!'

We **hurried** back to Grandma's mobile workshop.

'Excellent work, boys,' Grandma said. 'You did me proud!'

'Can you quickly **zap** us back to normal size, Grandma?' I asked.

'Sure!' said Grandma. 'I tinkered with the size converter while you were battling Dr Kane. I think I've finally perfected it!'

We hoped she was right! Grandma aimed the size converter at us once again . . .

ZAPPITY-ZIP-ZAP!

We were normal size again! Finally, the size converter did what it was supposed to do!

We got changed, rushed back to the bus and made it just in time!

EiGHT

As soon as we got home, we told Mum about our **MASSIVE** day. Mum was **proud** of us for saving Duck Creek again. But she was very worried about the Ultimate Ninja's fall.

'I hope he wasn't badly hurt,' Mum said.

'The way he looked at me . . .' I said. 'I'm sure he's my dad.'

'I think so, too,' Mum said. 'I'm so happy he's alive, but I hate that he's under Dr Kane's control.'

'How am I going to bring Dad home if he doesn't even know **who he really is?'** I asked.

'You'll find a way when the moment's right,' Grandma said.

She seemed so sure!

'What are you going to do with the size converter, Grandma?' Kenny asked.

'I've decided to retire it,' Grandma replied. 'But before I put it away, I did a few last tests. Come and have a look!'

We all went out to Grandma's workshop. When she opened the door, **we couldn't believe our eyes!**

'Looks like I can make you boys your favourite - **giant fruit salad!'** said Mum, laughing.

I looked to Kenny. We both had HUGE grins on our faces. Sometimes, being Ninja Kid and H-Dude is pretty cool!

READ THEM ALL!

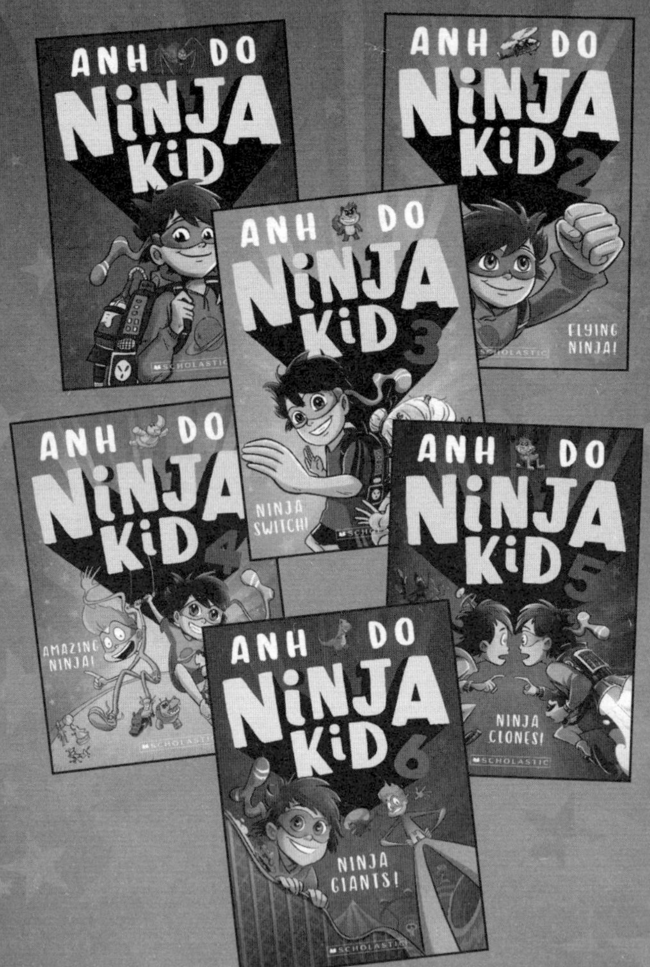

NINJA KID 7 COMING SOON!